First SCIENCE

WEATHER

By
Steffi Cavell-Clarke

KidHaven
PUBLISHING

Published in 2018 by
KidHaven Publishing, an Imprint of Greenhaven Publishing, LLC
353 3rd Avenue
Suite 255
New York, NY 10010

This edition is published by arrangement with Booklife Publishing.

Designer: Evie Wright
Editor: Charlie Ogden

Cataloging-in-Publication Data

Names: Cavell-Clarke, Steffi.
Title: Weather / Steffi Cavell-Clarke.
Description: New York : KidHaven Publishing, 2018. | Series: First science | Includes index.
Identifiers: ISBN 9781534523920 (pbk.) | 9781534523937 (library bound) | ISBN 9781534524804 (6 pack) | ISBN 9781534523944 (ebook)
Subjects: LCSH: Weather–Juvenile literature.
Classification: LCC QC981.3 C38 2018 | DDC 551.5–dc23

Printed in the United States of America

CPSIA compliance information: Batch #CW18KL: For further information contact Greenhaven Publishing LLC, New York, New York at 1-844-317-7404.

Please visit our website, www.greenhavenpublishing.com. For a free color catalog of all our high-quality books, call toll free 1-844-317-7404 or fax 1-844-317-7405.

PHOTO CREDITS

Abbreviations: l-left, r-right, b-bottom, t-top, c-center, m-middle.

Front cover – iofoto. 2 – Sergey Novikov. 4b – Kenishirotie. 4r – dencg. 5 – Asier Romero. 6l – Konstantin Aksenov. 6r – Evannovostro. 7tr – belkos. 8l – Elenamiv. 9 – Rohappy. 10 – PJ photography. 11l – nattul. 11r - sayhmog. 12 – Wolkenengel565. 13 – FamVeld. 14 – Vadym Lavra. 15 – Romrodphoto. 16 – Robert Kneschke. 17 – Suzanne Tucker. 18 – Clari Massimiliano. 19 – aaabbbccc. 20 – AC Rider. 21 – idiz. 22l – Hurst Photo. 22r – RTimages. 23 – Guas.
Images are courtesy of Shutterstock.com, with thanks to Getty Images, Thinkstock Photo, and iStockphoto.

CONTENTS

Words that look like **this** can be found in the glossary on page 24.

Science All AROUND US

What should I wear when it is raining?

What is weather?

How many types of weather are there?

Science explains many things that happen in the world around us.

What Is WEATHER?

Weather is all around us. There are many different types of weather. For example, the weather can be sunny or cloudy.

The weather is not the same everywhere. It can be cloudy in one area of a country but sunny in another part of the same country.

SUNSHINE

Never look directly at the sun.

When there are few clouds in the sky and the sun is out, we say that the weather is sunny. The sunshine feels warm on your skin.

When it is sunny, people often spend time outdoors. Most people wear light clothing to keep themselves cool.

It is often sunny in the summer.

CLOUDS

When there are many clouds in the sky, we say that it is cloudy. A cloud is a large group of water **droplets** in the sky.

There are different types of clouds. Clouds that float high in the sky are often thin. Clouds that are lower in the sky can look fluffy.

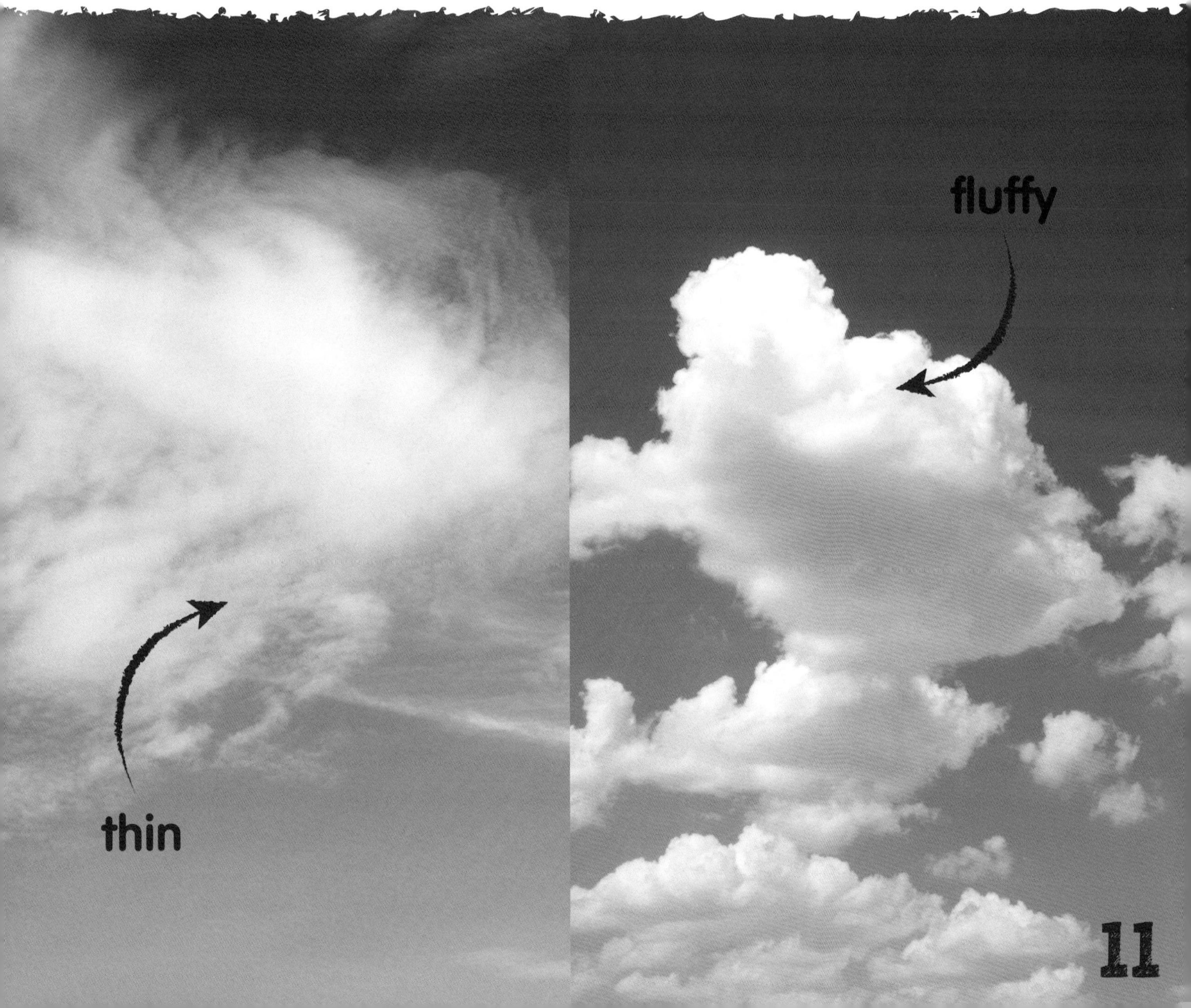

RAIN

When it rains, many water droplets fall from the clouds. Sometimes, clouds make a lot of rain, and sometimes, they make none at all.

Many people wear rain boots and carry an umbrella when they go outside in the rain.

Umbrellas are **waterproof**.

SNOW

It snows during the winter in many places.

When it gets very cold, water from clouds can **freeze**. We call the frozen water snow.

It is important to wear warm clothes when it snows. Many people wear hats and gloves.

WIND

Wind is air that moves around the planet. You cannot see wind, but you can feel it.

Wind can sometimes be very strong. Sometimes, wind is so strong that it blows down whole trees.

A strong wind is called a gale.

THUNDER AND LIGHTNING

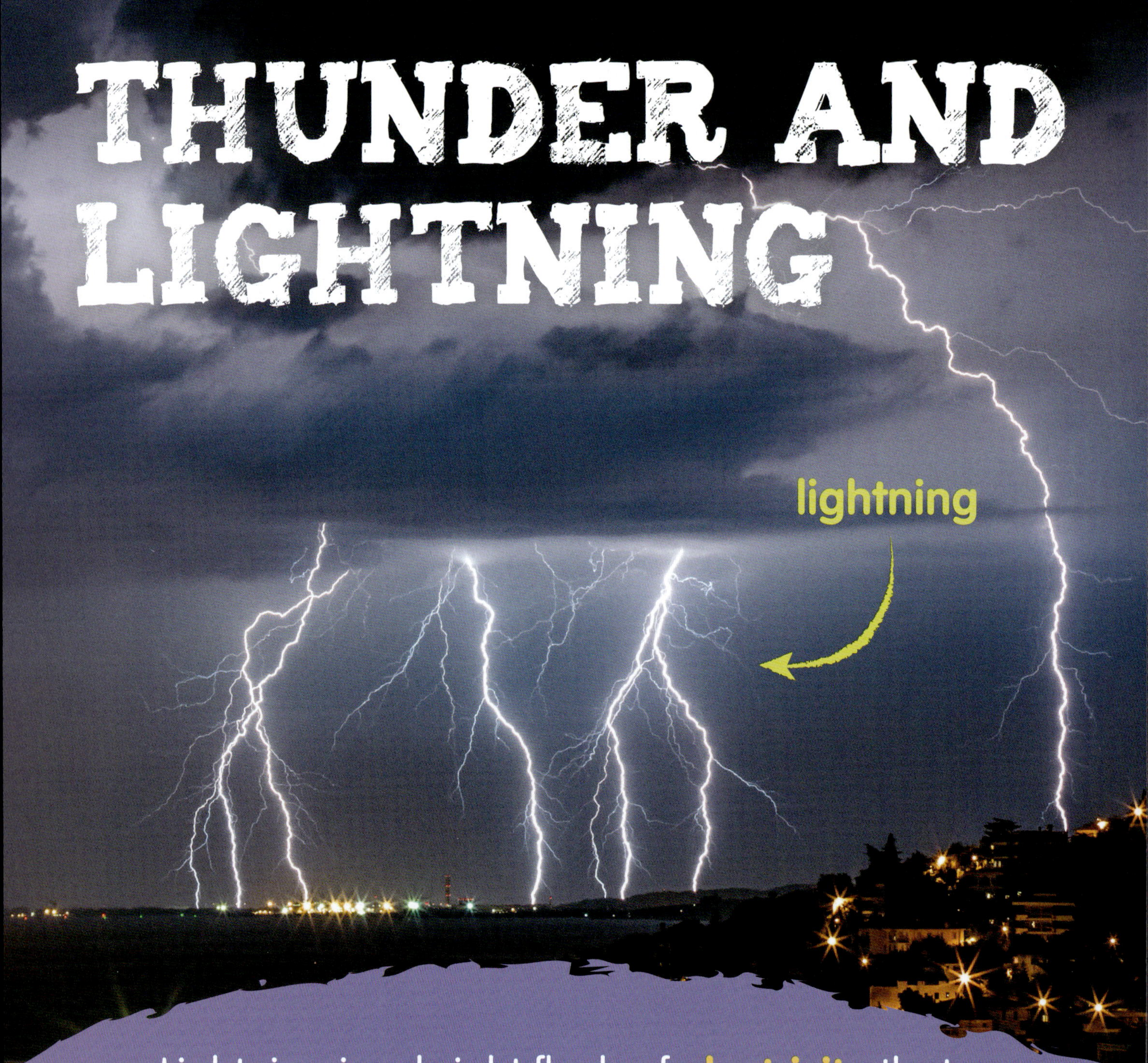

Lightning is a bright flash of **electricity** that generally happens during a **thunderstorm**.

Lightning makes a sound called thunder. Thunder can sound like a sharp crack or a low rumble.

EXTREME WEATHER

Weather can sometimes be dangerous. Heavy rains can cause **flooding**. Flooding can destroy homes and farms.

A **drought** happens when it does not rain for a long time. When there is a drought, rivers can dry up and leave many places without water.

Let's

EXPERIMENT!

How do clouds form? This experiment will show you!

YOU WILL NEED:
glass jar
plate
hot water
ice cubes

STEP 1

Get an adult to pour 2 inches (5 cm) of hot water into the glass jar.

STEP 2

Cover the jar with the plate, and wait a few minutes.

STEP 3

Put the ice cubes on top of the plate.

TOP TIP:
Ask an adult to help you!

RESULTS:

The cold plate causes the warm air inside the jar to make water droplets. This is the same thing that happens in the sky to make clouds.

GLOSSARY

droplets small drops of liquid
drought a long period with little rain
electricity a type of energy
flooding dangerous, overflowing water
freeze to turn to ice
thunderstorm a storm with thunder and lightning
waterproof resistant to water

INDEX